THE MAGICAL WORLD OF

BENNY AND BUZO

The Magic of Confidence

Written by: Manmeet Narang

Illustrated by: Suman S. Roy

Benny was learning a poem for the class assembly.
'Bob went with his rod,
to catch fish in the pond...'

Benny was finding it difficult to learn the lines. He looked at his stuffed toy Buzo sitting on the chair. He had an idea.

'Kazooka Bazooka, Ding Dong Ding!' Benny said the magical mantra.

Buzo jumped from the chair into the air. He began to swing like a monkey from the fan.

Benny and Buzo scratched as if they were both monkeys! They danced on the floor laughing.

'Buzo, please do some magic so that I learn this poem,' said Benny.

Buzo wagged his tail fast. Soon there was a drum set in the room.

Buzo played the drums and Benny began to sing the poem. In the end, Benny knew the poem well.

'Benny, now you have learnt the poem. Recite it well on stage. Best of luck!' said Buzo.

'No! I feel afraid on stage,' said Benny.

‘Come on! Be confident Benny,’ said Buzo.

‘Buzo, can you do magic
and make me confident?’
asked Benny.
Buzo was thinking.

'Zooka! Zooka! Confidooka!' Buzo said a magical mantra. 'Now recite your poem,' said Buzo.

‘First he caught an old mop,
Then he caught a broken top...’
Benny was feeling confident.

'You are my best buddy Buzo!' Benny hugged him.

'If you feel afraid, just say the mantra—Zooka! Zooka! Confidooka!' said Buzo.

'Benny, all the best!' Mom wished him in the morning.

Benny was feeling afraid to stand in front of the mike. He repeated the mantra 'Zooka! Zooka! Confidooka!' in his heart. He felt better.

'...Then he pulled out his rod,
It's a fish, thank God!'
Benny recited the poem very well. All the children clapped.

‘Excellent!’ the teacher hugged Benny.
‘You were so good,’ Mom patted Benny when he went back home.

Benny rushed to his room and hugged Buzo.

‘Thank you Buzo for making me confident,’ said Benny.

'But I did not do anything Benny. No magic can make you confident,' said Buzo.

'Buzo, you told me a lie!' Benny was angry.

'If I had not lied, you would have never believed in your confidence,' smiled Buzo.

'So it means I did it all by myself!' Benny jumped in joy. He hugged Buzo tightly.

Buzo winked and said,
'If you feel afraid, don't be,
You can do it, believe me!
Zooka! Zooka! Confidooka,
Just say these words, and then
you see!'

Activity Time!

Complete the scene of Benny's class assembly.

New words

poem

assembly

difficult

idea

scratched

learnt

recite

stage

luck

afraid

confident

feeling

mike

lie

believed

What did you learn?

What was Benny trying to learn?

How did Buzo make him learn the poem?

What was Benny feeling as he stood before the mike?

What had Buzo lied about?

Magic of Confidence

Teaching children manners and inculcating values in them is a task that requires immense patience. Feeling nervous and shy to face an audience is common in children. As they grow up, they become even more conscious. So boosting faith and confidence in oneself is crucial. 'You can do it' is a mantra which, as parents, you should follow to encourage your child.

Children can relate to the experiences of the characters in the storybook and as they read along, it leaves an impact on their impressionable mind.

Read out the story to your child with expressions and bring out the characters alive. Do answer any question that your child asks, no matter how weird it may be. Read out to your child the story, especially on the day he/she shows lack of confidence, and you will be surprised to see how magically it works!

More Fun with Benny & Buzo

9788131919811

9788131935569

9788131935583

9788131919835

9788131919842

9788131935576

9788131935590

9788131919828